LAMMAS·ALANNA

LAMMAS·ALANNA

WILLIAM·MARTIN

A convoluted harvest
LONNEN

BLOODAXE BOOKS

ISBN: 1 85224 369 4

First published 2000 by
Bloodaxe Books Ltd,
P.O. Box 1SN,
Newcastle upon Tyne NE99 1SN.

Bloodaxe Books Ltd acknowledges
the financial assistance of Northern Arts.

ACKNOWLEDGEMENTS
'Six Island Sunset', 'Midwinter Song' and 'Song of the Cotia Lass'
were first published by Taxvs Press. 'I Johnbird' first appeared
in *Dogberry*, and 'Bairnseed' in *Poetry Book Society Anthology 2*.
'Midwinter Song' was broadcast on *Poetry Now* (BBC Radio 3)
and was also set to music by the composer John Woolrich,
for tenor, horn and piano. The song 'We meet at the lamp'
along with other verses was set by John Woolrich; they were
performed at schools in Gateshead and were published as
a poster by Gateshead Libraries and Arts.

Cover printing by J. Thomson Colour Printers Ltd, Glasgow.

Printed in Great Britain by
Cromwell Press Ltd, Trowbridge, Wiltshire.

To my dear wife Win
and to our grandchildren
Georgia-Elizabeth, Stephanie-Ann,
Rachel, Daniel and Natalie-Jane,

and to the memory of Dick Fee
(1930-1998)
and Gordon Brown
(1925-2000)
I'll miss those bonny lads.

Busk ye busk ye my bonnie bonnie bride
Busk ye busk ye my winsome marrow.

W. HAMILTON, *The Braes of Yarrow* (1774)

CONTENTS

AFOREWORD

1.

Dorado full sky
Reflects in her water

Naked verbum immersed
But coming again to us
With words and the gab
Made golden

It is a cry
Out of beginning

A seed to the harvest reaped

A heart-beat
Of the spoken

2.

Swim internal
Seed implanted
Noisy workings
All the while

Then come the stirrings
Dark Eden expanding
First out of Ark
In deluge to dry land

A deep rooted tree
And dove-guide
Through stress land
With promise of
Foothold made hold

3.

A nativity accentor
Sings in the branches

It is word–flesh music
Heard first early morning

Giving praise
At the wonder
Of her bright
Herald star

A sign of beginning
A spuggie testament

HITCHYDABBER

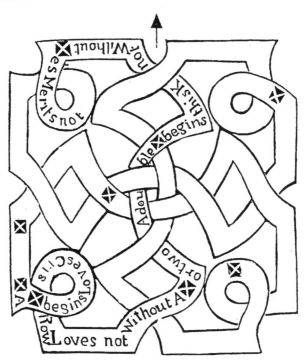

FOR the TREE of the G ABBALAH

FIRSTGATE

So now yer knaa how aall the folks on byeth sides o' the wear lost lots o' sheep and lots o' sleep and lived in m'tal fear... so let's hev one to brave sor john that kept the bairns from harm... saved coos and calves by makkin halves of the famous lambton worm

MORT·TIAMAT

Remember me o remember
me said tiamat. I am our
dream for all living and
dying. I am the seed in the
ground and the shoot and
the harvest. come gather
together when the moon
is a sickle and the field is
a golden sea. But the ✝
LORD spread out his net
to enfold HER

He called up the evil wind
He let it loose in her face

When she opened her mouth
Fierce wind filled her belly

Her body was distended
And her mouth wide open

He bent back his bow
And released a great arrow

It cut into her side
Splitting the heart

She struggled for life
But soon it was gone
He stood on her carcass

The Lord
Stamped on the legs
Of Tiamat

With his unmerciful hammer
He crushed her skull

When the arteries
Had been cut
The North Wind
Bore them away

He heaped up a mountain
Over Tiamat's head

He formed hills
On her breasts

He pierced them to make rivers

Her tail he bent
Across the sky

A Milky Way remembrance

Remember me

Her voice
Cried over the waters

Remember me

She thundered
In the sky

Remember me

She gasped in the black rock
Crushed underground

Remember me

In the Spring of the World

PSALM

I went into my lost love's place
Our Eden is enchanter and golden rod

I ate the fruit
Of my lost love's death

Our Eden is Devil's bit
And smooth sow thistle

I spat out the seed
Like Solomon's seal

Our Eden is Mountain everlasting
And small fleabane

I touched the pale root
Of my lost love's face

Our Eden is Tree of Heaven
And pellitory of the wall

QUEST

It is a Cockerooso hop

A singing interlaced path

A long way to Tipperary myth

A hardness of the heart
We struggle with

A self and other selves

Not one without the other

A Jack shine the Maggi to follow

A Bethlehem harvest now

HITCHYDABBER

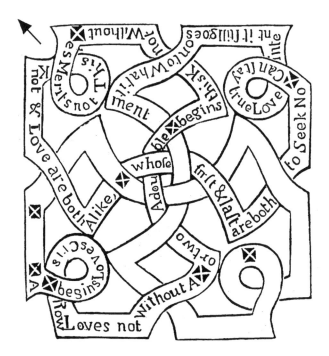

FOR the TREE of the G ABBALAH

DEATHFALL

CHANT

When the mistress of sparrows
Entered this house
When the mistress of kestrels
Stood at the door

Did you dress the bride's head
Did you kiss the cut corn
Did you nail the box lid
Did you chant her death song

Blind on the road
Her secret army
Blind in the bed
Her secret love
Blind in the bush
Her secret bird-call
Blind in the mirror
Her secret blush

GRENDEL'S MOTHER

A monstrous creature was grieving her loss

Grendel's mother lived in deep water
Doomed from ancient times
To inhabit the wasteland

The region was mysterious
Of wolf-wind and fell path

A water torrent from dark cliffs
Plunged into underground flood

The tarn lay overcast
No living man had seen its bottom

Multitudes of creatures
Were seen in the depths

They boiled with anger
As Beowulf fired an arrow

It stuck in a fierce throat

Plunging into deep water
And back again
The strange beast
Was caught by barbed spears
And brought to the cliff top
In wonder

Beowulf put on his mail-shirt armour
Figured and vast on his bone framed chest

A silver helmet encased his head

It would strike down brightly through deep water

He held in his hand a sword now lent to him
Tempered in blood and battle
It had never failed

The Geat then dived through steel-grey water

Waves covered the brave warrior

It took almost a day
To reach the bottom

Where the ancient flood-guardian
Saw humankind coming

She grabbed him with terrible hooks

But no harm could come
To the body under rings

She set out to drag him to her lair
In such a hard grip his sword-arm was pinioned

Throngs of beasts attacked
Ripping tusks
Tormenting monsters

Forced to the enemy hall
He saw in firelight blazing
The size of the Great Hag holding him

He forced out his sword-arm
And struck her a blow

The blade did not bite
Its sharp edge had failed him

Furious he flung it to the ground

He went for the Monster's Mother
Seizing her shoulder

Knife in hand
She promptly reached out to him
The mail-coat shielded his life
Barred point and edge
Saved him from death there

He got to his feet and saw the victory sword

This wonder would equal any battle-play

A giant's forge had fashioned it

He took the hilt
And brandished the weapon in circles

Shaking with rage
He brought it down on her neck

The blade sheared her bones

The Great Sword was gory

Light glowed in her chamber
As he searched the dwelling angrily
With his weapon held high
Seeking out Grendel's remains

The champion found him
With life gone out

Wounds gaped open

Sword swinging he brought it down
To cut off the head he prized...

High above Geats and Danes watched the pool

They watched and waited
Till blood came rising

They gazed in sorrow
And prepared to leave

But he swam up through water
Now clean and free
From otherworld creatures

He came to the surface
His silver head gleaming

SHARD

Version of an old Irish poem

Here is a song
That stags give tongue
In winter snows
After summer goes

High fell winds blow
When the sun is low
Its brief day song
In sea tossed throng

Bracken clumps hide
Red under white
Geese rise up
With accustomed cries

Cold encircles
Massed wings of birds
In the icy time
Bitter season's rhyme

BALLAD FRAGMENT

And round and round
The bonny bright hill
She coiled her speckled skin

She slept on the mound
The bonny bright mound
And all around were still

*

Still light on the river
And on the gold corn
The valley was blessed and one

The moon hung over
Her bonny bright mound
They waited for the dawn

*

The morning star
Bold herald of dawn
Appeared on the eastern bank

The sun shone into her treasure hold
Larks rose up with morning thanks

*

Into that glad day
The blade man came
He cut the laverocks down

He divided the treasure
Into big lots and small
And cast her bleeding
Into the tide-full river to drown

CAROL

Show us the way to Bethlehem
From Ynyswitrin to the sea
Show us the staff in ancient time
That flowered a winter tree
Show us the black helebore
Wax rose of Agnes called
Show us the way to Bethlehem
To Bethlehem to be born

Show us in brittle December
Light falling with the leaf
Show us the touch of Thomas Mass
Doubting the sun to sleep
Show us the face of the guizer
With Oozer hair and horn
Show us the way to Bethlehem
To Bethlehem to be born

Show us the way to Bethlehem
Out from the Yule tree leaf
Show us the way to the cradle
Acorn hand rocking away grief
Show us the way to the stable
With mistletoe and holly thorn
Show us the way to Bethlehem
To Bethlehem to be born

HITCHYDABBER

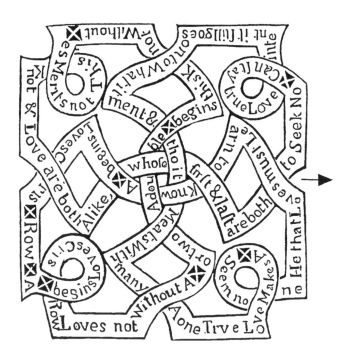

FOR the TREE of the G ABBALAH

✝HEAVENFIELD✝

CAEDMON'S
✝ HYMN ✝

Now should we praise
The Guardian of Heaven's Kingdom
The Maker's might and his mind's thought
The works of the Father of Glory
How he Eternal Lord
Made a beginning of every wonder
The Holy Shaper
Built Heaven a roof first
For men and their children
Then
Mankind's Guardian
Eternal Lord
He afterwards made earth for them
That Lord Almighty

I · JOHNBIRD

images found in and around the book of wearmouth

LIGHTKNIFE · cuts
cake-dark hole
GOBBLING us and pandect
figures painted along
shore say that from
✝ beach-gloom of the
codex there is no end·:-
no end to spuggie
swallow after hall
and solstice struggle
no morning in the
morning they say

2.

Day faces west gazing in majesty

Throne stool ringing
Four khaki walkers
And humming flyers

With pink under grey clouds
Even now true

And uncials beginning and end
Old and new together

3.

This lot we plodge

Barefoot Evangelist's eagle
Our wing over grey swell

For now we see
Horizon cliff and cave mist

And pebbles turning forever
To beach dust

Clinging between toe's print
And infilling ingrown
His nail-pain washes away

4.

They skim flat stones
Crestfallen to drag

And search again wittingly
Lord stones rolling over Holey Rock

His risen water
Tide high up face mark
All my days he said

Today and yesterday
With rain then hail

For who knows the Kingdom weather

5.

Again he waves to them
Empty skies rain spent

White horses wouldn't drag
More wild spray he rides

Going keel over
Grave-drink-briny
The dead coral

His heel black birds wake after
Scavenging sea worms
In tide decay

6.

Dark in thorn tree dark
Birds blossom

Its spikes winter bares
His night thoughts
Roost among them
A shuffling nocturne ritual

But who is here
And the Lord risen

7.

He whispers behind us
When bank gravity
Lightens our step

And dark increases
Our going over the hill

He is shadow maker
Even in shadow

He is dream light
We hardly grasp on waking

His memory
Squeezing out of hand
As we grope
Heads jarping Easter in our ears

8.

Yolk sticky
We shiver for shell crunching

Waiting fluffdown
And put away chick things

I Johnbird
Haven't seen the eagle I am
Except carved or painted
But I feel air now
Hissing feathers close by
In this dark hangar
We wait to fly from

9.

I will spitfire
The counted sparrow heads

And rake
Mustard seed fields
I Johnbird

With winged Matthew man
And look
Lion flyer leaping bull force

MAY·TIME

From the Black Book of Carmarthen

Kintevin
Maytime
Fairest season

Yoked oxen plough the furrow
The sea is green reflecting
Fresh colours clothe the earth

When cuckoos sing on fine tree tops
My sadness grows

Fire-smoke stings

At night I am restless
Since my loved ones have gone

On hill and in hollow
On islands of the sea
Everywhere you go
With the White Christ
There is no place forsaken

Seven saints
Seven score
And seven hundred
Have gone with the White Christ

There is no dread there

A favour I ask
Please do not refuse me

May I have peace
May I find the gateway to Glory
Among Christ's people I should not be sad

SCORDIE

1.

Plain hermit Cuthbertus
In east end splendour

Bede outside the
Blocked west door

Carved Apocalypse words
His Morning Star Christ

Crucified upended Peter
On faint Galilee fresco

The old fisherman
Ladder top at foot
Fixed with Roman nails

2. (Amiatinus)

Three times fivehundred beast skins
To a slaughter of pandect

Sixhundred his crossbrood
Kiss farewell

CEOLFRIDIS ANGLORUM
EXTREMIS DEFINIBAS ABBAS

The desert movement
Smudges ink here

Fingers will not write
For northern winter

3.

Lion-flame eaten
In Tunc-page Kells

Virgin folio like
Cuthbert's oak

But viridian and purple
Not simply incised

Saintly profiles in box frame
Jewelled dog-head seat

Angels with the
Look of Donovan

4.

Echternach's Lion Mark
Leaps after fledgling

Chad's carpet writhes
Like a stone turned over

Out of tangled genealogy
Kell's Jesse sprouts

INITIUM blossoming

CHIRO full grown

5.

Durrow beasts in interlace
Bite cased Wearmouth stone

Pictish manuscript-slabs
Thumbed by all weather

Gospel book 'fashioned for
God and Saint Cuthbert

And all the saints
In Lindisfarne'

Orange relic sun
Crossbrood trooping west

6.

Durham Gospel fragment
Matthew's ending recto through skin

Crucifixion in A.II.17
Interlace confusing angels

And spear bearer
And sponge bearer

Are my burning eyes
(Folio thirty eight)

The Lord's last flare
Fading on vellum

TRINITY

From the Black Book of Carmarthen

Who is two
And who is one
And who is three together

Who is it who weekly
Makes Tuesdays and Mondays

Who made man
And who made woman
Their shadows and depths
Are not one

Who made hot and cold
With sun and moon forever

Who made a wax letter sent
A flaming wick shaking shadows

Who made fruit
And who made seed
And love of a bonny lass gentle

THE·DREAM·OF
✝THE·ROOD✝

WHISHT! I dreamed at midnight
When Mankind slept

A dream of dreams
I will tell you now…

I saw the tree high in the air
A beacon clothed in gold

Gem-stones flashed
Angels flocked to gaze upon it

Not there for thieves to hang on
But a sign of Victory

✝

The tree shone with Heaven gold
Gems sparkled for the Maker

Yet behind the glow
Signs of suffering showed

Nail marks and bleeding
Pity in the heart

✝

Afraid I saw the brightness change
From golden warmth to cold haling sweat

It was spattered with blood

Sorrowful I saw the Healer's Tree
Best of wood it spoke to me

My mind goes back
To the copse
Where they cut me down

I was hauled off to a roadside

Others with adze and saw
Made a rood of my wood

✝

Soldiers carried me to erection
On a hilltop
Enemies all around
Then I saw him coming towards me
Mankind's King
Bravely to climb upon me

✝

Naked he came
Eager to mount
Unafraid
Facing them

He would free Mankind
He embraced me but I dared not bow

✝

They hammered dark nails
Through deep wounds into me
I was lifted up
A cross for the Great King

They mocked us
I was wet with blood from his side

On that hilltop I saw the Lord stretched out

Clouds wrapped him

Darkness on the King

All Creation wept
Keening his death

Christ was on the cross

✠

Friends lifted him
Down from pain

Gazed on the Lord
Singing their grief

Under the Tree of Death
Our Bringer of Victory

✠

I stood there weeping
Till his enemies felled me

I dreamed in the earth...

At last I was found
By the Great King's men

They adorned me
With silver and gold

⊠HITCHYDABBER⊠

FOR the TREE of the G
⊠ABBALAH⊠

> ⊠ TIDEROAD ⊠ >

EXILE

At the ferrystones I left them

Their river-wrinkle
Showed no reflection
Of vessel and grey band gathered

Only gold of the cross glowed
Brood all around it
Not a hand said farewell
When my ship-drift
Sought the break-white bar-gap

Now it is Friday and the fishers beach
Hauled out headland seals
Wail in blue before chanters

I am over rock and across sand
An exile white beyond the bar

THE·SEAFARER

I tell a true story
A tale of myself

Sitting all day at the oars
Gripping against sorrow

In bitterness I steered my coble
Among endless cares

Bows through tossed foam
Watching for cliffs
Numbed with night falling

✢

Sea-weary
Cares hungered my heart

Cold gnawed at my feet

No happy man can guess on land
How I wandered without kin
Marraless in frost

✢

There was bitter hail
And sea birds' lonely call

Not men's laughter
Gathered together

But gannet splash

Sharp beak in my heart despairing

✢

With friendship
Life is sweet

Warm around hearth
They barely think
Of the banished man

At nightfall
Weary at sea
In snow from the north

✛

Thoughts come knocking
Of a great sea crossing

Again the mind moves
Soul seeks the way

Over wind-water fetch
To new people far off

✛

No man is so wise
Before going
Who does not think over
Where the Lord leads him now

Not dwelling on trinkets
But her delights put aside
Only sea-waves in eyesight
Salt tears at her loss

✛

Green forests and farms
Communities thriving

Urge the eager to voyage
To fells fresh growth

Where the cuckoo calls
Herald of summer

But sorrows still throng
In the midst of his song

✢

What happy man can know
What hardships come
Who sail in spray
Far from land

The cuckoo's sound
Drags me across water

I remember the Lord's kindness

I do not believe
Earthly things
Are everlasting

Three things threaten our peace

Illness or age or vengeance
Shall draw the breath

But praise well won is lasting

Men and angels shall honour it

On good lips it shall not die

✢

Days are soon over
When a leader fails

There are none like those
Whose good deeds
Were the World's first

Our songs honoured them

But excellence grows old

Age greys and thins the head

We cannot lift a finger

It is no good laying
Up treasures on earth

That cannot allay
The Judgement of God

✢

BEDE'S·GOING

Migrating wings take him

I inked these flat birds
Like Lindisfarne pages
After gifting his Cuthbert book

I was there
I took the north lonnen
Waded Don then at ebbtide

Had I heard they said
Only hours since he worked
And hours to that journey
All must make

'No man is so wise
Before going
Who does not think over
What good or evil
His soul will be judged'

He said

SIX · ISLAND SVNSET

1.

Blue-eyed Evangelist
You came in skins
To this treeless island

Jack Eagle Evangelist
You roost
A stone bird now

The beginning word
You brought
Is lapidary light

Green lichen
Gems cold pictish boss
Unforbidden child on the cross

2.

West kindles beatitude
The earth shall inherit

It was before the fire
Brendan left ring of saintly pebbles

His footstep dissolved
His keel deep in shingle

But the heretic sunset burns
Rack centuries southward

3.

Paul with stone head
Wept long for his brother

The Lord of sunset
Is taking names

A star-maiden's foot
Dances on water

We call her Bridie
The white daughter

4.

They welcome fiery angel

Virus sword of all horizons

Lord give us this day

Their parliament discusses
Fish eggs and sheep
Who sink or swim with common boat

5.

Returning again
She spoke out of currah

Blue net from her mouth

The crowd stood with dunlin
And weed jumble

Words garbled in surf

6.

High golden star
Between my eyes
St Kilda burns
Be wise be wise

High golden star
Cold Pentecost tongue
She burns afar
The sea is dumb

High golden star
Who speaks for men?
The west is red
Amen Amen

THE·DREAM

From the Black Book of Carmarthen

I had a dream of the sea last night

Shrewd would be the interpreter
Of its seeming wickedness

Only I was witness
Others will not know

(Leading a host is a fine thing)

We were under the same blanket
This young lass and I

She was the colour
Of waves among pebbles

(Working for the good is no tribulation)

I walked into her
She opened her arms in the spray

We moved with the sea
Coming up and down beach sand

We seemed to be endlessly rocking...

But at last she was gone
Gone in my wave crash...

It is still on me

(Whoever does wrong frequently
Will be finally overtaken)

HITCHYDABBER

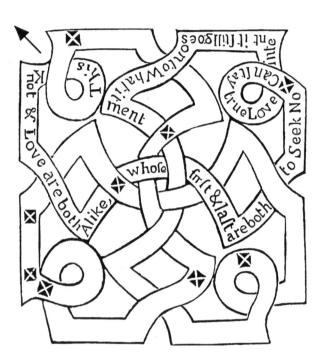

FOR the TREE of the G ABBALAH

DREAMRISE

BVTTERFLY

My spick-bonny love's like a haystack pin
Butterlowie let
Butterlowie light
She spilled my passion blood
Nicked my finger ring
Butterlowie light
Butterlowie let
Will I find my needle-hinny?
Butterlowie light
When the blood-wound's healed
Butterlowie let
I searched the buzzing air
For her laverock song
Searched the cowslip meadow
For her secret nest
Searched the dandelion sun
Butterlowie let
Nearly lost my sight there
Butterlowie light
For my spick-bonny love's like a haystack pin
Butterlowie light
Butterlowie let

MIDWINTER
·· SONG ·

1.

Longshore Feneris rives

Gale splits on groin

White curtain drench

Bricks and flint
Sheep and goats
Granite in the teeth

Stand up
The storm
Unleashes
Counting

2.

Remember the kiss
Of first rain before Ragnarok

A lark in meadow grass
And flowers
Her hair almost covered

Pollen-nose
And buttercup reflection
Yellow cheek

3.

He said the meek
Would inherit

Stood there
On this hill
Where his mother
Met a stranger
From Hope Wood

And he met another
That first summer

4.

And the blessed thing
Won't lie down

It won't lie down
Stars finally witness

Even the moon
In its last dying
Testifies Bethlehem

5.

I will go and no more
Said wince to sickle
I will go and no more
Said cry to wind
I will go and no more
Said deep wound to throbbing
I will go and no more
Said hurt to steel

6.

This back end
May be the last

Have you seen my
Bonny lad limping

Last year's child
His ear now close to earth
Waiting the first squeak of green

7.

Are you coming
To the woodbine
To the nip
The drag
The swallow

Are you coming
To the nettle
To the blister
Pain and rue

Are you coming
To the kissing
To the sorrel
Dock and yarrow

Are you coming
Adam handed
To her cree-play
Eden school

8.

I do not wish
The moon to lag
Come to the fields

Or the sun to
Sleep the caller
Come with your poppy-flood

I do not wish the
Cock to un-crow
Over dyked barley

9.

Farmer farmer
May we cross your golden river
May we cross your golden river
In our silver boat?

I will call out the colour
Of the one who'll cross my river
Who will cross my golden river
In that silver boat

IN·EAST HOPE

1.

I will awake
With your eyebrows
Grey-brown
Almost touching me

Then breathless push you away
As image mates object
Searching

Trees will say yes with strange noise
And birds
(Is it yellow the blackbird bill)
Like liquid mass

Must her eyes
Her eyes
Her eyes

2.

Clouds appear
Over the head of the hill

Blue is going I heard it said

Wrinkles soon darken
The brow watching

And blue is broken

Cracked patches of it falling
Till nothing
Nothing remains but cloud
At the head of the hill
And waste broken blue
Lying in the fields
Surrounding

3.

The dying blossom in heaps
Like dead flowers cast away

Red and white blossoms

And the sea shivers light
On its rippled surface
Over to islands
Those black islands
Looking into the sun

The same sun that
Rises and sets on us

And her flesh is soft
Under the arm
Next to her breast

4.

I heard a man
Killing his sky
When Paradise passed

His gore-cry
Under snout-crowd thunder

Daisies wept blood
On Paradise passing

And children

Swept from cliffs
Thudded to sand cast up

5.

Always when new rain
Bursts its droplets
Against glass

Or is felt tapping flesh
To trickle and be smeared

Always then I should remember
How it seemed to fall free
Returning to us

6.

From once a mill hill
Mist hides hollows
And orange ball is half in haze

Barley wet sunset
Cream snail crossing road
Over spilt blue pattern of paint

No scarecrow's tattered wooden cross
No ghost-red sails
At pylon's end

7.

Orange girl
You are dyed in sunlight
As I pass
Your feet in shoes
So delicately held together
Waiting

Orange girl
Orange girl
Birds are stained too
As they play the wind
Wings stiffly sailing

8.

Crows I saw
And may dying

But summer sang naked
And wind
Barely a breeze
Warmed her waist
Till I came

When sentinel beeches
Stood west of us

And rust nestled in blossom

SONGS·FOR THE·LADY OF·CHAPELGARTH

1.

I dined on the road
To my lover's
Sweet fenced in bed

Drank the road wine
To my sweetheart's
Black hood edged in red

Smelt the perfume
Of the flower
She kissed that grey morning

Saw the dark cave
Love was blinded
With first and last crying

2.

I remember the star
Jewelled star
Rising on her breast

Milky Way hem
Milky hem
Lifted to her neck

Orion hands at her waist
Belt there undone
There undone

Twice from her moon face
The open-armed cry
Will you come

3.

It was down by the river
Reflecting her swelling
I saw her

The eyes of a child
Dropped three tears
Deep drowned in her waters

With her crown on his head
He slimed from her frowning
His Kingdom foot held up high

I give you the end
Of her golden cut thread
Cut to his dying

4.

He died and he lived
In the skull of her bone head
Socket-light orbit

He lived and he died
To the touch of her hand
Like a feather-bone wish

He died and he died
With the kiss of her bone lips
Brushed aside on cheek

He lived and I lived
On the road to her fenced in bed
Lighting her wick

5.

She was the Whore of Revelation
Burning lamps in seven churches

The black-damp underground
Pressing kisses into
Eighteen inches

The Beatitude coming down
On our blessed eye-lids touching

The darkest dark blade
Dying corn sees
Hand grasping ripe bunches

6.

It was down by the
Swirling liquid birds
Touching trees into chorus

White frost-shadows
Reaching for words the frozen tune fits
Melting for us

The lowie in summer insect haze
With silent delicate touch

The lost love in her chrysalis hood
Green energy stripped into pollen dust

HITCHYDABBER

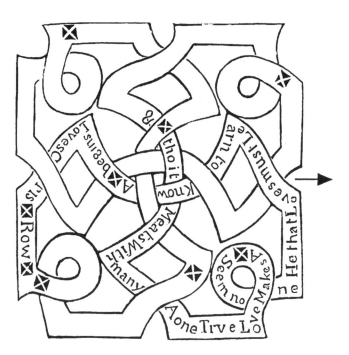

FOR the TREE of the
ABBALAH

ΘLADYWELLΘ

SHARD

Take me
To the mountain

Take me
Over the stile and away

Bring me into the Silver City
The Silver City will tarnish today

Find me yesterday's sheaves of corn there

Find me the sickle
Rusting green

Rest my head
In the midday cradle

Touch my quick
With yesterday's seed

IMAGES·FOR SAMVEL PALMER

1. *The magic apple tree*

I walked in this valley
Of the magic apple tree

I talked to a piping shepherd
Stooked corn tumbling down

I ate a red apple there
Full branches bending over

I touched the steeple pointer
Gold-tipped among barton ricks

2. *Cornfield by moonlight with evening star*

Waning moon
Touches the corn
Ablaze now

Scribbled hills
Her breasts uncovered

I walk the path
Between
With staff and dog

A star overhead
Comes through cloud
To follow

3. *Harvest moon Shoreham*

He stands with arms outstretched
As the others stoop

Greeting the haloed moon
Resting on a wooded bank and cliff

Purple sky and massed leaves
Nestle the red roofed
Church and steeple

Strewn corn is on the ground
Thrown after their sickle-arm sweeping

4. *A rustic scene*

Moon's shadow hangs
Among fruit from a tree

Vision valley light there
Reflecting between hills

Corn ears celebrate
Like fist-seed clenched

Ploughman drives his team and plough

Unyoked sweat drenched oxen
Look out

5. *In a Shoreham garden*

It is all blossom above
As she floats at the end
Of this garden path

Cabbages and beans
Border with
Sweet peas and onions
Through and under against green

Red and white garment

Pink and white blossom

The smell of her going

The smell she has left

6. *Early morning*

They huddle under a tree in corn
Our ancient children waiting

Yellowing eastern sky
Pushes her shadow
Across grass and rocks

A hare boxes the dark back

A dandelion clock
Waits for her morning lip breath

He loves me not

He loves me not

He loves

LADY·OF·THE SWEET·X·KISS

'Panayia tis Glykofilousas' at Petra Lesbos

1.

Lady of kisses Lady of rock

I circumambulate
The phallus base

It is proud out of green plain

Cockcrow and white horsetail swish
Spattered red poppies
And dove cooing from poplars

Sea still as the tranquil moment
Ejaculation gone

2.

The amplification of morning prayers
Coming across olives

One hundred and fourteen
Steps to her blessing

Helpers heave the lame
Blind touch carved edge

Meek seek beatitude
Her kiss for all people

3.

She looks over pantiles
Hooked into roof shapes

It is every day under them
The little ways forgiven

Down narrow lanes
The trivial are blest

Settlements high on the hill
Overlooking

Rock proud in May sunshine
Fishers returning
The sacred meal prepared

4.

I kiss you again in the wind

This cool alleyway shade
Blue ended by sea

There is no other way
None other than earth

Bells ring for us all
As the meal is shared

HITCHYDABBER

FOR the TREE of the G ABBALAH

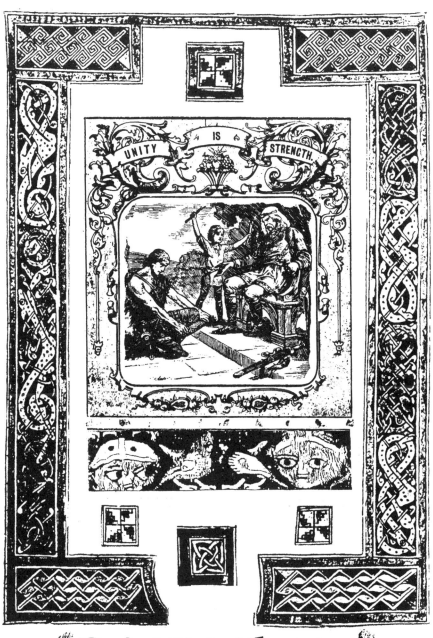

UNITY IS STRENGTH.

BAIRNSEED

PIECE

I hopped in the morning
With this hitchydabber stone

I was called in to dinner
With my plenker in a hole

I climbed an early afternoon
And smoked a goldleaf tree

I fingered her first
In our Eden-cree dark
Went blinking in to tea

BAIRNSEED

*These twenty-six streets were
within the wall of the original
mining village of Silksworth*

1.

Aline Lord Robert
Quarry Maria Hill

Remember the evictions there
In eighteen ninety-one

Remember the candymen
Slipping the greasy stairs

Remember the cayenne pepper
As they moved their bits o' things

2.

Londonderry Silksworth Terrace
Split by the school

Girls in the west black yard
Eastern side lads bool

On the mountain stands a lady
Skip the turning rope you two

Mountykitty one
Leap one two three
Mountykitty mountykitty
Fall off me

3.

Edward Stewart Frances
Doctor Hopper's bones

Run down the black path
Keep ahead of stones

Baked bread on window-sills
Flat-cake fadge and loaf

A whole street of baking days
Draws bairns by the nose

4.

Cornelia Tempest Vane
Twin middens across the road

Precious loves and prize leeks
In black garden soil grown

Vane Arms for argument
Maughin's shop alone

Glass-ally kids in back lane
Making their way home

5.

Castlereagh Tunstall
Wynyard William John

West end and east end
All within the wall

Fish shop and cropper
Beasts to their fall

Father brings us chocolate
From the I.O.G.T. Hall

6.

Seaham West Henry
Charles North Mary George

Mother's chapel my chapel
Say my "piece" rehearsed

Grandmother Mary
And Grandmother Jane

Big Meeting banners
Coming up the lane

SONG

1.

We meet at the lamp
And watch the moon
The end of the world
Is coming soon

CHORUS
What shall we play
On Vinegar Hill
Hitchydabber say Hollycarrside
Let's hoist the banner
Let's mountykitty
Let's skip let's tig
Let's dress the bride

2.

Mam's got Jesus
Dad's got Marx
Eve's got me
In the wash-house dark

CHORUS
What shall we play
On Vinegar Hill
Hitchydabber say Hollycarrside
Let's hoist the banner
Let's mountykitty
Let's skip let's tig
Let's dress the bride

3.

Don't knock the props
Off Armstrong's wall
He'll clip yer lugs
And keep yer ball

CHORUS
What shall we play
On Vinegar Hill
Hitchydabber say Hollycarrside
Let's hoist the banner
Let's mountykitty
Let's skip let's tig
Let's dress the bride

4.

Mackerel Mackerel
From out the deep sea
Don't follow Polaris
To Elsie and me

CHORUS
What shall we play
On Vinegar Hill
Hitchydabber say Hollycarrside
Let's hoist the banner
Let's mountykitty
Let's skip let's tig
Let's dress the bride

5.

Stephen Arkley's
Dad's a puff
His mam smokes a pipe
His gran takes snuff

CHORUS
What shall we play
On Vinegar Hill
Hitchydabber say Hollycarrside
Let's hoist the banner
Let's mountykitty
Let's skip let's tig
Let's dress the bride

6.

Robin redbreast
In a bright cage
I missed school once
Or twice
And the School Board man
Wrote page after page
To the Committee
And me poor mam
Had to see the Chairman
Who raged like Heaven

CHORUS
What shall we play
On Vinegar Hill
Hitchydabber say Hollycarrside
Let's hoist the banner
Let's mountykitty
Let's skip let's tig
Let's dress the bride

DURHAM BEATITUDE

The Easington Colliery disaster in 1951
remembered at the Durham Miners' Gala

Gorse blazing on clifftop
I saw three ships
Thorns and May blossom
Explosion at pit

Saul's Dead March
Common grave and grief
Beatitude their banner
Weeping and drum beat

A gentleness flowered
In each drum silence
A Kingdom confronted
Each green thorn

They that mourn
Came here in July
Field blessed with banners
Thronged comforting hush

I saw three ships
Through the gorse sail in
They came to Death's harvest
They came to pulley-wheels

SONG

As aa was gannin
Through Chester-le-Street
Three canny women
Were mackin a feast
They had a stew-pot full
It bubbled and squeaked
As aa was gannin
Through Chester-le-Street

As aa was gannin
Through Houghton-le-Spring
The same three women
Were hevin a fling
They louped ower dyke tops
With a kite on a string
As aa was gannin
Through Houghton-le-Spring

As aa was gannin
Through Pelton Fell
Three bonny women
Were ringing a bell
A cat with a fiddle
Was up a-high singin
As aa was gannin
Through Pelton Fell

As aa was gannin
Through Hetton-le-Hole
Bairns were dippin
Their crusts in a bowl
The women kept fillin it
Aall the time fillin
As aa was gannin
Through Hetton-le-Hole

As aa was gannin
To old Durham town
The three canny women
Were dancing around
With skirts out like banners
As bold as brass sound
As aa was gannin
To old Durham town

HITCHYDABBER

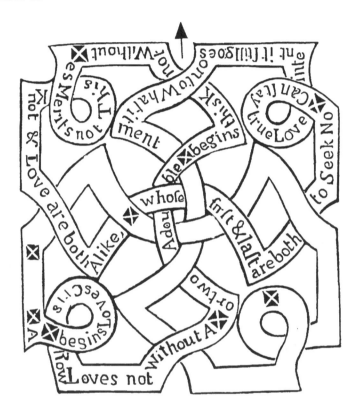

FOR the TREE of the Ϭ
ABBALAh

MAGGILIGHT

SONG

Jack shine the Maggi
Cry Jack shine the Maggi
Follow her Jack's Maggi light
Into dark
Jack shine the light in her
Jack shine the Maggi
Shine again Jack in the dark

Will dayligone fash
Or be egged on in fettle
Its bleezer laid idle
Claes hoyed forgetten
Will neet louse its bairn
In forst heed the caaller
In hadaway neet-time
The morn's morn's nigh hand

We'll rise up aall soakin
Like babbies out o' watter
We'll gan to her gatherin
Each one a marra
We'll tack the wide lonnen
It's nee good the narra
In hadaway neet-time
When the morn's morn's nigh hand

Jack shine the Maggi
Cry Jack shine the Maggi
Follow her Jack's Maggi light
Into dark
Jack shine the light in her
Jack shine the Maggi
Shine again Jack in the dark

HIS·BRIGht SILVER

(SONG)

Traditional

The bonny pit laddie
The canny pit laddie
The bonny pit laddie for me O

He sits on his cracket
And hews in his jacket
And brings the bright siller to me O

1.

Pit yackers dance to
Pulley-wheel buzzer

At Kelloe the calf hill
Chipped cross-face of Helen

At Hetton and Elemore
Trimdon and Esh

Little Chance is the gallowa
Putters all bless

2.

Beech candles drip wax
Into root-fibre cutting

Full draped bier
Draws empty one up

On twisted steel rope
On gravity bobbins

As children whirl haloes
Discarded hemp-core lit

3.

Stephenson's steam theodolite
Spies lay for waggon line

Lambton Hetton and Joicey's logo
Bold on wooden sides

Wheel-squeak and larks
Sing along with fossil birds

Embanked through bowed reapers
Eden's last harvest falls

4.

Brick warren estate
Rabbit Wood overrun

High rise shadow blade
Has steel cord cut

Ghostly crossing keeper
Muffler clay pipe and spit

Old "face" now "bank man"
Like Hefænricaes Uard
Dreams and puffs his twist

5.

Hazeldene evensong
Church on green edge

Sunset banner
Starboard tapers lit

Deep bramble harrowing
Chancel-bow dip by Gox

Pit-head Malkuth
In bent barley

6.

Memorial words
Uncial Quarter seam

Bonny May morning
Night shift on the face

Telltale yellow cagebird
First shift in the Gate poor lads

Black explosion banner
Stone names all but one

7.

Candles flicker in eviction tents
What Kingdom without common feasting

When they were seated
Silk banners on fellside

Friends after nettle broth
Turned slogans into bread

By the poor for the poor
They taught themselves

8.

Street children cry Cockerooso
Generations hop across

Spuggie chorus crack
Cathedral choir sing anthem

'Our feet shall stand
In thy gates O Jerusalem'

Larks rise with brass
Big Meeting last one for Eden

9.

The bonny pit laddie
Sits on his cracket

Corf fill the keel
Keel fill the brig

Dark drift or shaft hole
He hews in his jacket

And brings the bright silver
The canny pit laddie

His eye full of silver to me

SONG OF·THE COTIA·LASS

1.

The keel took my heart
In full tide it was torn
The keel took my heart
Black blood to his flame

The waggonway fall
Was braked by the river
the horse on its tether
With nose-bag and corn

The keel took my heart
To whistle and wo-lad
Down in his brig of dust
Down to his hot ash breath

2.

On lip of drift crying
I sang the raa up and down
Black the craa hinny
Ivvry day now

I sang over fell where
Grey pocked my
Green stitched hem
Smouldering sway there
Banners to brighten

The keel bought my heart
It was bonded and bound
The keel took my heart
In full tide it was torn

3.

Who rose in the morning
To see the keels row then
Who'll rise in the morning
To see the keels go

It was down by the river
Ventricles pumping there
Shute and flat bottom
Leveller schull

Who rose and who'll rise
With banners and drum thump
The keel took my heart
Silk over it laid

4.

The keel played at morning-tide
Bide and abide with me
Keel-brass for my heart blown
Banner-water bidding

Rite blinds were drawn to
Down staithe banks drawn all the way
Hats doffed and held there
In the ebb-tide hush

Down in yon forest
The keel rang my heart away
Black bells of Paradise
Hutton and Harvey change

5.

Foy-boatman blow the flame
Loosen his rope-fast sail
Scorch the wind southerly
Fill it with fire in flood

Blood rages over bar
Out in the molten toss
Fury and friend are lost days
Where you are

The keel sought my heart
In full tide it was torn
It beats every tree on fire
Wagga-pulse fossil dawn

SONG

A Wearside version

It's O but aa ken well
Ah you hinny bird
The bonny lass of Pennywell
Ah you Ah
She's lang-haired and bonny-fyaced
Ah you hinny bird
With gold and silver on her breast
Ah you Ah

Hetton line comes ower the top
Ah you hinny bird
Waggons bound for Lambton Drop
Ah you Ah
Peter's for owld Bede
Ah you hinny bird
Chapelgarth sunk in a field
Ah you Ah

There's Pans Bank for salters
Ah you hinny bird
And Hope race-track for halters
Ah you Ah
Hendon for taarytowt
Ah you hinny bird
And Silksworth pit for 'aall out'
Ah you Ah

There's Backhouse for artists
Ah you hinny bird
And Old Vic pub for Chartists
Ah you Ah
There's Roker front for bonny lights
Ah you hinny bird
Jack's Maggi shine for dark nights
Ah you Ah

There's Tunstall Hills for Maiden Paps
Ah you hinny bird
With lovers lying in the grass
Ah you Ah
There's Tid Mid and Miseray
Ah you hinny bird
Carlin Palm and Paste-Egg-Day
Ah you Ah

There's Doxfords and Pickersgills
Ah you hinny bird
Riveter's and plater's skills
Ah you Ah
There's collier brigs and keel row
Ah you hinny bird
All gone out in the big tide flow

Ah you Ah

ABVBA·BIDE

1.

Her ground heaves farewell
Heaps of love-fire sent

Bleezer encourager
Drawn over black lead

Sunday cracks the word to us

Crackle-cone on mantel
Rakes pew-less hymns
In memory ash

Blazer flickers in corners
Shadow-arms gather us
We are counted

2.

Her dene calls out to us
From nettle beds
And young sycamore shrubs

She calls from the no-go
Trespass land
Over the sharp fenced division

Gray beech boles either side

Sixpences a secret treasure the sod hides

A run across meadow slope
To get the breath back
At her well

3.

Maggi light lit briefly all night
As they move around in darkness

The mysterious dene
Has lovers abide there
Till eastern blue
Brings distant bell across fields
To slate roof of Aline

Where children all fall down

Their ring a ring broken
To her bell sounding

For she's the only one

Wallflowers growing up
All the precious time away

4.

We walk the colliery line
To a canyon quarry
High on the edge of her breast

Glimpses of masturbation
In Hope Wood

Pitch and toss
By Gamblers' Rock
As we pass

Girls and boys going on
To nothing much

Scrambling up loose limestone

Just a fumble among
Orchids and cowslips
Then home

5.

The engine steams its way
With long train of empties

Bairns on battery sides
Watch brake van tailing off

Their fathers are
In Mothergate
Down under

The buzzer has called out
A click click of heelplate reply

Baccy cigarettes and matches
Are hidden in hedge holes
Edging the black path
Leading down

6.

There is a hill not far away
Where love divine is given

Where tender mercies come to fix
In this our humble dwelling

It is a song of rising bread laid out
Like the word fresh baked to eat

But when is the day
That the fish man comes
When is the day of the fish

Callerherrin! Callerherrin!
Street by street he cries

How a' yer the day misses
How a' yer me hinny
Come buy my Callerherrin
You'll thrive

7.

Cockerooso! Cockerooso!
Cockerooso! my side

Then they all hop across
With much dunching of shoulders

And many a foot put down

Which means that they
Join with the caller
Out there in the middle ground

Where she'll call out another
If he crosses right over

To cry with a loud
Cockerooso! come on!

8.

Tid Mid Miseray
Carlin Palm
Paste Egg Day

We sing our rhyme
Counting the weeks
To Easter Morn rising

Some say it is not
Christ we sing about
But the old Earth
Which has given us birth

We roll none the less
And all shout as they go leaping

Then we jarp

9.

Her hill-breast flesh
Glows above corn ripening

She oversees the harvest coming soon

We play around climbing the Rocky
Or rolling down tender grass slopes
To a strip of strong blue sea
Smudged with chimney smoke

Colliers sailing off
Leaving her emptying mines behind

10.

A bouncy tram takes us to the beach
After walking down lovers' lane

The stream yellow with colliery waste

Her lovers embracing in bough shade
Bring whispers under hand
As fresh blood begins to rise

But we are soon off on the top deck
To eat gritty sandwhiches in a circle

And to chill our scrotum in the sea

11.

A song comes into the ear
From somewhere about

It is marra music that gets louder
Brass voices tenor and bass fill the morning

And its beat bloods the heart
Of many following

She is singing in long streets
Calling all like the piper

But not to be lost

It is a way of arms linking
A dance of life

12.

I didn't know her then
As I went to the front to be saved

The preacher had called
To us all to come forward

My mother and grandmother
Treated me like a saint at suppertime

But she calls now in a different way

Just look at her Lammas breasts
And deep vulva dene

Bairns play there often
It is a different passion

HITCHYDABBER

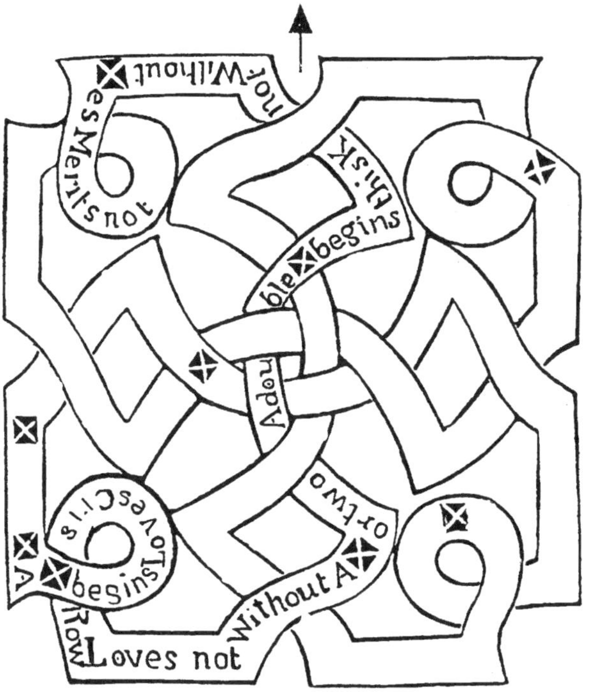

not Without
es Merit's not
this K
ble begins
Adou
or two
A begins LovesC is
Row Loves not Without A

FOR the TREE of the G ABBALAH

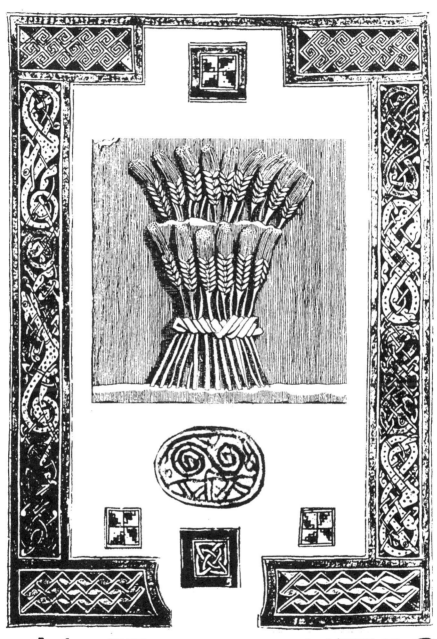

MOTHERGATE

many are the days gone
after so long away
returning
reading the words afterwards
doing the things
helping to restore
after all its place was taken
really
mothergate
one of its deep roots
always

MOThERGATE

1.

Romanesque solar worms
Rising and setting

Fruit from the mouth
Of the eastern man

Chipped out miracle fishes

Ark birds and assorted
Biting and apocalyptic beasts
Spew over the arch into western jaws

2.

Walkaway eastern man
Whistles her tune down from stone

He sings the fruitful mouth flow

Green songs sprouting
Sap rhythm dancing

Tongue and lips tasting
Melody going out

3.

He stumbles behind the song
Stone eyes slowly made flesh

Stiff joint to supple hinge
Quicker than sandstone thought

He picks himself out of the pebbles
They crunch under his flexible sole

4.

He waves in at the first turn
No way straight ahead

Loose dog rose petals
Fish-scale the path

They ruffle at contraflow
Each lift speaks to nostrils

Ripple-scabs and cat-fish eyes
Round the curve
Intestinal twistings on the way

5.

He walks east by convolution
Sole blood rises

Eyes shot with dust kicked up
And off from township rejecting

They close their ears
Stare behind palms
Rush him to the outskirts

6.

Stones follow his path
Clenched fist left behind

They speak the way
Impelled down bank

It is narrow but not straight
Eyes rolling round bend again

Heat haze reflecting
Warning shot out of sight

7.

Bright ventilation hole
Sound coming down

Unaware voices rattle on cobbles

They recede into past
Memory jolted by new light ahead

Recurved lustre
Grow-shiny walls
Own face distorted

8.

He turns away from his apparition
Twisting on heel

Goes unsteadily hung across Mothergate water

Moulded 'Nil Desperandum' there

Cantilever arching
Over limestone gorge
Incised meander

9.

Sea smells curve from
Headland book to headland book

Birds in blue borders
Constrained by gold frame

White legs interlaced
With legs of another one

Feathers connected by
Overlapping wing beat

Common air flow lifting the pages

10.

His feet mark the shoreline

Rose out of reach
Pricking inner finger

Washed up menstrual blood
Caking on rocks

Wader red to joint
Scarlet gannet breast
Moon face covered

11.

He faces her roofless
His cry lost in refraction

His mumble of dead
Lost meaningless repetitions

Fading script jargon

False gold leaf curling
In scrolls around the walls

12.

He is tangled
He inhabits the vine scroll

He nests among branches
Waiting for her in notches
Cut with expectation

But dropping to the floor
Flaking out under foot

13.

He is become angel
Wings drying in wind on rock

Humming gusts harp wires
To proclamation unto you

Shepherd of flock birds
Bringing the to-fro tide
With cross-stitching legs

White hem-power flowing
Touching marram hands

14.

Grass is foundation against wind
Green holding on to touch-and-go sand

Red Fescue Lyme and Couch
Corn-Sowthistle Sea-rocket Frosted Orache

Wheatear in Buckthorn
Bush spiking air

15.

A chain they dance
They sing a game

Wet sand between toes
Root of their hands held

Cord-haired flower stem
Proud seed in his wind again
Stork's Bill under child's head

16.

I went out late to live in her tune

Feet pressing it in
I was yesterday him

He went and he goes in the fret damp sun

Unrolling her tune
It was yesterday hers
Dancing over screen words

17.

He sang along with them all
Mouthing her syllable bounce

Good song and bad song
All taken into count

Foot notes and hand chords
Touch the strings heart frays to knot

Tied up in twisted hemp
Weak bound with strong

18.

He walks into doubtless
Before diaspora

Is it timelessly common
From her primal Eden walking

Is it stripped of adornment
Is it proud now to angels

Is it guiltless and fruitful
In her chamber of entry

19.

Who goes into the dark
In the dark of the deep dene wood

Who goes hand in hand with her
In a clasping stumble down

Who will touch the arrow
The arrow and the heart fresh-carved

Who will sing for the moon out now
Who'll sing in the silver dark

20.

We go down into her

Mothergate arch depicts
Scenes of beginnings

Hunter-gatherer hand
Passing around
Meat morsels
Root chewings

Nut kernels shell cracked
And placed on the tongue

21.

Candles smoke her
Black face blacker

False-gold clothing over
Old-young shoulders

They stumble suddenly

Face to face whispers

Goaf-void prostration
Trailing behind her

Lone touching shovel
Embryo fossil hand
Polished steel

22.

Even the inverted mountain air
Shivers with cold sun stored in her bed

She cups the everyday wordless servings

Articulate motions
Body language connections

Web over her cave without a centre

23.

We enter without touch
Queuing the man-rider

Belt endless or seemingly
Just for a moment

No wearing out
No stopping for stale breath
On the return

No black tears seeping
Up to bait and bottle niche

24.

Long lost Jordan River
Profuses her blood

Extravagant horsetail logs
Crashing to carbon

Segments dating her

A wing fan delicate and flattened
Wafts downdraft smoke

Brass mantelpiece pole and velvet skirt
Drawn above blazer hand

25.

Missed spit sizzles on grate iron

Every hit briefly darkens

A sunspot like blotch
Quickly reheated

Revival breath channelled

Fierce sucked air drawn
Cock-sure towards her

Newsprint paper singeing to flame

26.

Before the scattering
Handful of seed

Before the secret dawn
Before germination
Blackness now in

Before blade
Slicing wind
To the day

27.

Heard rooks swarm
Then fidget into silence

Heard the uncertain wind

Heard the shell's sea roar
Head-size in his hands

Heard the exponential cry

28.

Uncertain the wood
Night birds upon stone

Uncertain the rocks

Hedgehog yellowhammer
Blue-tit dog

Uncertain the light

Every feather every quill
Uncertain the fire

29.

Who will cry

The greatest of these is cast out

Will you split the wood
Lift the stone
Throw the seed

Will you select the best fish among them

Invite all and sundry to the feast

30.

I met a maiden (brown)
It was all in the garden

I touched her eyes (so blue)
It was all in the blackfall night

She was wed in the garden (green)
It was all in the morning

A ribbon was tied to her hair (gold)
Go up the hill and dance

31.

Night and the stars
Behind her eyes dreaming

Rapid eyes like the flicks
Frame by frame sprockets hauling

A fleeting vision

The spool near its end
Ready to switch

32.

He said yes to her golden hair combing

Yes to her coble hauling the fish

Yes to her haven rocks
Hidden choir howling

Yes to the morning bell
Her clapper swinging blue

33.

Who is coming to her Bethlehem harvest

Will fish flop ashore
Scales drying in grit breeze

Leaping at sand hills
With hopper and kelp

All heaped up in chorus
Strata-gills taking breath

34.

It is every day waiting for the end

All stand up for the last image
Without thinking much

It is coming soon the trailer said so

Monday Tuesday Wednesday
Or Thursday Friday Saturday
Coming soon

35.

If I cry Cockerooso now
Generations will hop across

If I wait for the banner coming home
Everyone will rejoice

If I cross the golden river
It is the colour of going

If I rise with sheep and kye from my bed
It is ever so bonny at morn

36.

Hawk on a stick as the ship sails into her
Fish hidden behind in the golden skim

Drowned stalks flicker
A hungry look-out wakes

Flashers still finger the leaving dark over

37.

In the silence of waves
Reaching apex on sand slope

In the dream condensing
Here on hard rock

In whisper footprints
Turnstones surge up and down
And are lost in the draining

In being ready for the some day
Sharing natural and wanting

38.

The seed was cast
By the sower's machine

A mound in the midst
Like her belly swollen

Lights and noise and dust
Collecting her fruitful

I break her bread in remembrance
Her stick of life

39.

Her chapel hymns harvest seed
Ranting in fields

Do you take this sheaf of child
This straw-rope umbilical
From oats-loaf oven
Fresh bleeding bread broken here

Take this and remember
Flat cakes cooling on window-sills
Schoolboys sniff Bisto-style

Yes and backlane alleyholes
They plenker their way daily

With pockets jingling
Hopscotch and hitchydabber
Till Cockerooso they all hop across

40. SONG

Dreaming on her shapely

Dreaming on her belly fire

Dreaming on her birth pangs coming

Dreaming on her Marradharma now

        * * *

Dreaming on her broken waters

Dreaming in her golden corn

Sailing on her harvest ocean

Dreaming in her Marradharma now

BACKWORD

1.

Rape gleaming in mist
Large expanses illuminating

Sickly stink where
Corn grew sickle handed

Summer moon
Labouring over stooks

Fossil seed with bait
And bottle fallen

Midnight texts laid out

Counted loaf crusts
Tapped and golden

2.

I sing of her
Wandering herald star
Bright before
Blue appearing

No sleeping the caller
For anybody

Gravity engine grinding
The sun up before long
In the twinkling rapidly fading

Light years a blink
Like eternity in her eye

Kisses the breath of life
In extremis unthinkable

3.

In their multitudes
Universe on universe
Bright bones of Albion
She gives them birth

Her cry across immensity
And infinitesimal sighs

With the great kettle boiling
Both hereabouts
And ower yonder

She is labour forever
With echoes unending

NOTES

I was born in 1925 in a mining village three miles or so south-west of Sunderland. My mother was a Methodist, and on Sundays I rarely missed going to chapel three times. This included Sunday School. I was brought up on hymns and preaching, and lodge banners and the solidarity they proclaimed. But there was also the separate secret culture of the street. Games like Cockerooso, Jack Shine the Maggi, Mountykitty and Hoist the Banner were a great joy for the children of that time. There was little or no traffic. The gas lamps produced pools of light in the darkness. This was our contact with an oral tradition that enriched our lives.

I left school, aged 14, in the summer of 1939. After this it was a world of work and war. In 1944 I sailed for India in the troopship *Orduna*.

This work is laid out in nine sections or chapters (nine is the number of the Goddess) and with each chapter heading is a knotwork design with integral text. The text can be divided into three verses and there are various arrangements distributed among the nine. You have to imagine the nine designs can be laid out like a hopscotch or hitchydabber children's game, with an arrow pointing to the position of the next one to be hopped on. I also thought that with all the designs laid out it could look like the Jewish mystical diagram the Tree of the Cabbalah.

Ynyswitrin: The Welsh name for Glastonbury.

Tiamat: In Babylonian myth the Great Goddess Tiamat was destroyed by the God Marduk.

Kintevin: a Welsh word for Maytime.

Ceolfridis Anglorum extremis definibas Abbas: 'Abbot Ceolfrith from the furthest end of English soil.' Part of the original dedication page of the *Codex Amiatinus*.

I.O.G.T: the Independent Order of Good Templars.

Chipped cross face of Helen: The Romanesque Kelloe Cross is to be found in the Norman church of St Helen, Kelloe, Co. Durham. The sculptured designs describe the finding of the 'true cross' by St Helena in Jerusalem.

Wagga: light from hot slag tipped onto a waste-tip.

Mothergate: the name given to the main roadway in a pit.